BIGMAMA'S
Donald Crews

 Greenwillow Books, New York

For BIGMAMA,
Cottondale and
everybody there—
now and then

Watercolor and gouache paints
were used for the full-color art.
The text type is Futura Heavy.
Copyright © 1991
by Donald Crews
All rights reserved.
Manufactured in China by
South China Printing
Company Ltd.
www.harperchildrens.com
First Edition
25 24 23 22 21

Library of Congress
Cataloging-in-Publication Data
Crews, Donald.
Bigmama's / Donald Crews.
    p.   cm.
"Greenwillow Books."
Summary: Visiting Bigmama's house
in the country, young Donald Crews
finds his relatives full of news
and the old place and its surroundings
just the same as the year before.
ISBN 0-688-09950-5 (trade).
ISBN 0-688-09951-3 (lib. bdg.)
ISBN 0-688-15842-0 (pbk.)
1. Crews, Donald—Biography—Youth
—Juvenile literature. 2. Authors,
American—20th century—Biography
—Juvenile literature. 3. Country
life—United States—Juvenile
literature. [1. Crews, Donald.
2. Authors, American.
3. Illustrators. 4. Family life.
5. Country life.]   I. Title.
PS3553.R45Z465   1991
[92]—dc20
90-33142   CIP   AC

"**D**id you see her?
Did you see
Bigmama?"

We called our
Grandma Bigmama.
Not that she was big,
but she was Mama's
Mama.

Every summer we
went to see her—
Mama, my sisters,
my brother, and me.
Daddy had to work.
He'd come later. It
took three days and
two nights on the
train. Now we
were nearly there.

"Cottondale. Cottondale. Next station stop, Cottondale," yelled the conductor to the nearly empty train. "Don't leave no babies on this train." He made the same joke year after year.

SOUTHERN

My uncle Slank came for us by car. We always hoped he'd come with the horse and wagon, but he never did.

We crossed back
over the train tracks,
a turn or two along
the red dirt road, and

onto the lane in front of Bigmama's house.

Bigmama and Bigpapa were waiting for us on the porch. There were hugs and kisses and "Oh my, how you've grown!" and "How tall you are…is this you?"

Then off with our shoes and socks. We wouldn't need them much in the next few weeks.

Now to see that nothing had changed. In the hall, the sewing machine that you had to pedal like a bicycle. The big clock over the fireplace. The wind-up record player.

The kerosene lamps
and the Sears Roebuck
catalogs. Our room—my brother's
and mine and Uncle Slank's.
Across the hall, the room
where my sisters and
Mama slept. Next to it,
Bigmama's and Bigpapa's room.

Then to the back porch.

Off the porch were three rooms. The tiny extra room no bigger than the bed in it. None of us wanted to sleep there alone. The dining room with the big round table and chairs. And next to it, the kitchen. On the porch was the washstand, where we washed our hands, faces—and feet. At the end of the porch was the well. "Don't fall in," we were told every year. No one ever did!

We stood on tiptoe to watch the bucket go down and fill with water so that we could have a drink from the dipper that hung nearby.

Everything was just the same.

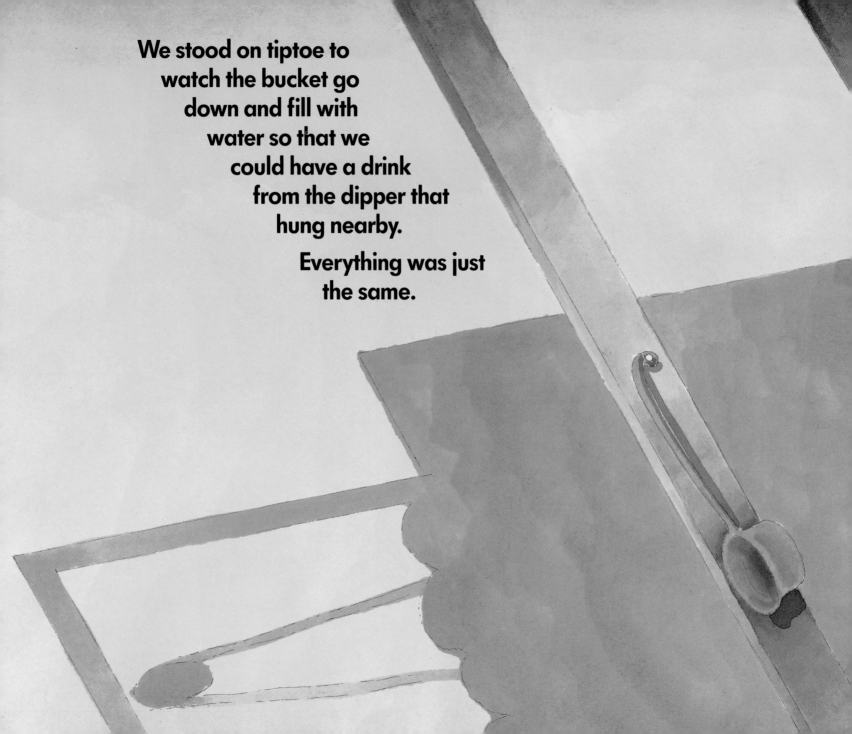

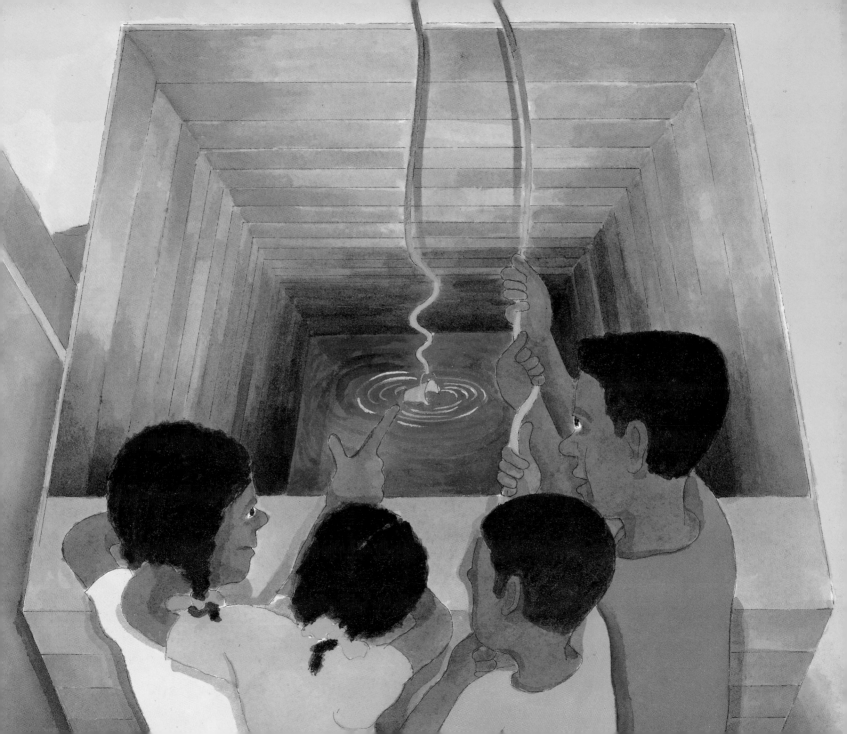

In the backyard
was the chicken coop,
where Sunday
dinner's chicken spent
its last days.

Behind the shed full of old stuff was the outhouse. Okay now, but scary in the dark.

We stopped for a drink at the pump.

We ran past the pear tree, where the turkeys roosted at night.

Under the tractor in front of the toolshed was a good place to look for nests with eggs in them.

Next to the toolshed was the huge, empty pot for making syrup from sugar cane juice. I dug some worms from the big pile of cane pulp. Wigglers were the best kind for fishing. I chose a pole.

The barn was another place to look for eggs.

On to the stable
to see Nancy
and Maude.
Maude was friendly,
but Nancy was a biter.

Down the path, past the cow pen and the pig pen, to the pond. The flat-bottomed boat was still there. Plenty of water for fishing and swimming this year. Everything just as it should be.

"A FISH! A FISH! I GOT ONE, I GOT ONE!" I yelled.

"W H O O... W H O O..." The train whistle. Dinnertime.

Everybody sitting around the table that filled the room— Bigmama, Bigpapa, Uncle Slank, our cousins from down the road, and all of us. We talked about what we did last year. We talked about what we were going to do this year. We talked so much we hardly had time to eat.

The night was jet black except for millions of stars. We could hardly sleep thinking about things to come.

Some nights even now, I think that I might wake up in the morning and be at Bigmama's with the whole summer ahead of me.